MW01000984

CIRCLES

A Legacy

CIRCLES

A Legacy

Susan H. Brown

Edited by Martha Fuller
Layout and design by Sharon E Rawlins

HERMANN PRESS
Encino, California
hermannpress20@gmail.com

ISBN # 978-0-578-67150-5

Printed in the United States of America

For Levi, Naomi, Maya and Benji
so they have a better understanding of their history

To Murray
with all my love

לנצח נצחים

CONTENTS

America 1969 – present

Parents

Mother and Father's Family

Cello 1943 – present

Appendix

CIRCLES

A Legacy

A LEGACY

The past sticks like old glue.
I set out on a voyage
That is yet nameless.
Tells of countries abandoned,
Always missed.
Languages learned,
Never forgotten.
I startle as gentle hands
Tap at secrets.
They offer love,
I sense their strength, their truth.
I love back. I trust. I listen.
I roam through pieces of my buried self,
I swim through dried up lakes of tears.
I open doors to secret stories.
I scoop it all up
And with my lover we put it back together.
The voyage brings me home.
The countries and languages left behind
So long ago,
Now here for me
To uncover lost wanderers' past.
Strangers' journeys
A testimony
For me to preserve –
Our legacy.

— PROLOGUE —

In 1947, Hungary was still in ruins from WW II and the new communist regime took hold. Raised by a Holocaust survivor mother and an ideologue socialist father, I learned to maneuver a tightly controlled social system as well as the loneliness of an only child.

In 1949, when the secret police installed a family in our apartment, I welcomed their young daughter as my playmate. I was unaware the family had been ordered to watch my mother after my father was falsely charged with treason and arrested. I didn't mind sharing our living space.

My nanny Annus provided the love my absent father saved up while in prison and the love my working mother had only limited time for. When my father was rehabilitated and returned home in 1954, I viewed him as an intruder. I resented my mother for taking him into our home and I competed for my father's love by idealizing him.

Following the Hungarian uprising, our family left for Vienna, Austria in 1957. I soon adapted to the new country, learned German and changed my name from Zsuzsi to Susi. Unlike Hungary, Austria still openly harbored anti-Semitism. When I started university, I began to shed my secret Jewishness, hoping that studying psychology would help me resolve the conflict of my identity.

My parents' decision to move our family to the US in 1969 forced me to adjust once again to a new culture and learn a new language. I also changed my name again — this time to Susan.

Struggling with many losses, I enrolled in university to study German and Yiddish. This proved to be a temporary solace until I fell in love. In 1972, I married Murray, a solid American Jew and budding psychiatrist, who understood the unspoken words I hadn't yet learned in English. His profound capacity for love, kindness and generosity helped me find an internal balance I yearned for.

With a final name change when I married, I combined my previous professional endeavors into a new career in speech/language therapy. Empathizing with children who fail to communicate proved to be a rewarding experience.

After many years of work and raising two daughters, I embarked on a new project with the Shoah Foundation. I translate Hungarian testimonies of Holocaust survivors and contemporary educators who fight anti-Semitism and all racist movements.

My mother would be surprised, my father would approve.

MY PARENTS' HISTORY

—

György (George) Hermann *1921–2015*
Márta Friedländer *1917–1997*

—

My father, a Jew and son of a wealthy merchant, grew up in 1930s Budapest, Hungary, a semi-feudal, semi-fascist country. As the only alternative to an unjust and anti-Semitic society, he joined the leftist youth movement. His father, a sophisticated bourgeois man, worried for his son who was filled with lofty ideals and sent him to Switzerland to study. Due to the law of *numerus clausus*, my father was prohibited from attending university in Hungary.

June 1938

In Zurich, Switzerland, my father quickly found a group of young exiles who shared his passion for a new worldview. He turned from a moderate socialist democrat to a believer in a humane communism. He traded his university studies for a career in journalism, disseminating his new vision in various Western newspapers. Living in neutral Switzerland, he managed to survive the war. The murder of his family, the murder of six million, and the murder of the hope for a democratic Hungary convinced him to return home and be "present at the birth of a better future".

March 1944

Germany invaded Hungary. Two months later my mother Márta, her father, sister and two-year-old niece were deported to Bergen-Belsen concentration camp. In June 1944, they followed orders to step out of *Appell* (roll call). Without an explanation they were herded, once again, onto a train. Filthy, hungry and scared, they silently held on to each other and to the illusion of hope. When they were taken off the train, the station identification Basel appeared as a *fata morgana.* Instead of German shepherds, German SS, German shouts and insults, German speaking Red Cross workers gave them food, hot water and beds.

My mother never found out how they, the four Friedländers got on what came to be known as "Kasztner's Train". Rezsö Kasztner, a Jewish lawyer from Budapest and shrewd businessman was determined to save himself and other Jews' lives. In one of his negotiations with Eichmann, he offered to free three hundred and eighteen Jews in return for hundreds of trucks, but the trucks were never delivered. In 1957, Kasztner was accused and tried in Israel as a Nazi collaborator. He was later assassinated.

My mother's experience in Bergen-Belsen reinforced her rejection of religion and she decided to stay in Switzerland. From Basel she made her way to Zurich where she met my father György, a young Hungarian refugee.

November 1945

Displaced, lonely, angry and distrustful of the future, my mother joined my father, the unscathed idealist. As soon as the borders opened, they returned to Hungary. With my father's idealism and the pressure of the government, she too joined the Communist Party.

July 6, 1949

The Hungarian Secret Police took my father away. By then dozens of the "Swiss Group" had disappeared. The truth of what happened in the next five years trickled in slowly. Beholden to the USSR, Hungary tortured, killed and declared all prisoners to be traitors of the government. Show trials swept through Albania, Bulgaria, Czechoslovakia, Poland and East Germany. These Stalinist purges in Eastern Europe ended with Stalin's death in 1953.

September 1954

After my father's arrest in 1949, my mother never lost hope that her husband was alive and continued her work as a chemical engineer. With Stalin's death, the political climate changed in Hungary and my father was released from prison on September 1, 1954. He began working in a publishing house, editing and translating German literature.

October 23, 1956

Hungary struggled politically until October 23, 1956 when the revolution broke out. Two weeks later, it was brutally squelched by Russian tanks.

February 3, 1957

A visitor's visa enabled us to board a train for Vienna, Austria.

HUNGARY

1947–1957

New Playmate

Two years old

I don't remember her name
I don't remember her voice.
She was my age.
She moved in with her parents,
Squeezed my mother into the living room.

My father away in a secret place,
Did *he* send this new family?

Using the wall in my room as a canvas,
My new playmate and I
Clutched our crayons,
We scribbled and giggled.
We never did it again.

Her parents' faces a blurred memory,
Their presence a mystery.

Years later I learned
That family was a pawn of the secret police,
There to inform on my mother
While her husband's secret place
Was a jail.

Sandbox

Two years old

The sand feels soft. I dig down in the brown, grainy mess. I scoop some up in my palm, fingers spread. I watch it rain down into my lap. Yellow bucket and shovel lay forgotten by my side.

The September wind blows my hair across my face. I brush it away but sand gets in my eye. I blink and rub and almost cry. I hope daddy will be here soon. I wonder if he is wearing his long black coat? Will he unbutton it so he can wrap me inside it as I walk next to him? I'll try to take big steps to keep up with him.

Or will he lift me up and the soft wool will warm my whole body? He'll hold me. I'll hug his neck and my kisses will indent his smooth cheek. His ear so close to my mouth I will whisper, "tell me a story." He will tell me about places far away, of people he knows, of things only he has seen. He will talk as we cross the playground, climb up the steps to the third floor to our apartment. While I am still in his arms, he will open the door and slowly glide me down the entry hall. We'll go in the kitchen and he'll make a sandwich just for me.

"Zsuzsika, come!" my mother's voice yanks me back into the sandbox.

I see her standing, so straight, lips tight, eyes dark green.

"No, I am waiting for daddy."
"Your father can't pick you up today"
I don't move. "Why?"
"Because he can't be here now."
"I'll wait."
"You have to come with me."

She sits down at the edge of the sandbox. My lips tremble, I don't want to cry. I move away but she grabs my arm, pulls me up. I swing my pail at her. She lifts me out of the sandbox. I kick, I scream – sand sprays in all directions.

She holds me tight, she says something but I can't understand her words. Tears and drool and snot drip down my face. I wiggle myself free of her grip and throw myself on the ground. I lie on my stomach, arms outstretched. I bang my head on wet hands, tears slip off with nowhere to go.

"I wait for daddy, I wait for daddy," I scream between sobs.

Five years later, he comes. He doesn't wear his black coat. He doesn't hoist me up. We stare at each other – we don't speak.

We listen silently to our own stories, stories that continue to grow for decades before they can be shared.

Black Pigs

Two years old

In October 1949, my father was arrested by the secret police. My mother sends me to be safe in the countryside at my nanny's home.

I swirl and turn, my new brown shoes blind with dust. The pebbles under my feet screech. I stop. Fear stomps on my chest. My hands at my ears push and squeeze — the noise an endless thunder.

Black pigs march toward me. I shut my eyes. Tears crawl down my neck. I look for help. Pigs stare at me. How many?

I turn. The door to the house is open. Jancsi leans against the sink. He holds the ends of a white towel that hugs his neck. He faces the little mirror so he doesn't see me. He doesn't hear my hiccupping sobs.

The yard is so big. The pigs now stand still, lined up, like the dolls on my bed at home.

"Where is my mother? When can I go home?"

Seven Years Old

My fingers bump across the chain link fence
Echoing my footsteps.
I listen to my lace-up shoes grind the gravel path.
With my classmates, I follow my mother.
We head home.

"Your father!" screams my mother.
I stop.
Curled around the cold metal,
My fingers hold me up.

My father?
With a hint of a smile,
He lives inside the yellow picture frame
On my mother's night stand.
He hides among a pile of postcards,
Once blank,
Now filled with letters of the alphabet
That march in a straight line.
He wrote those before I learned to read,
Working far away,
Over many years.

My mother runs,
A dozen seven-year-olds follow.
I catch up,
Climb the stairs.
We squeeze into the living room.

From the balcony
A strange man walks toward us.
He is silent.
He looks around.
He turns to my mother,
"Which one is mine?"

October 23, 1956

Nine years old

A fire in my schoolyard,
I watch children and teachers
Burn books, papers, red scarves.
Shrieks and laughter mingle
With fluttering Cyrillic letters
That turn into a rain of ashes.

Bewildered, unknowing,
I rejoice in the unexpected turmoil.
"A revolution," I hear all around.
A surprise holiday, schools closed,
Streets burst with people dancing,
Wading through fliers
Like snowflakes dropping from the sky.

Some weeks later a hush, like a cloudburst
Dissolves the crowds.
Tanks rattle on cobblestones,
Gunshots roar in the nowhere.
Confusion and questions whirl
Like dry leaves in the October wind.

In the cellar at night, three of us
Tiptoe upstairs to listen to the radio.
It doesn't play Bach,
It shouts words I do not understand.
Home now all the time, my parents whisper
And roam the apartment like shadows.

Hours empty with waiting,
Days filled with questions and unfinished sentences.
Secrets swarm like buzzing mosquitoes
I cannot catch.

The revolution squashed, the cellar empty,
Ordinariness returns.
I fumble for the familiar,
Learn to make new memories.

Fall slips to winter,
Steady snow muffles my parents' voices.
Their words, their faces a dark riddle.

My aloneness a warm blanket.
Its softness soaks up
My longing and dreams.

Annus

February 3, 1957

Ten years old

My forehead pushes against the cold glass. My arm reaches up, holds the top of the lowered window. The February wind bites my fingers. Sobs and spit dribble down the glass.

Annus stands on the platform. Her voice climbs up to me. "Don't cry *nyuszikám*, I love you."

Tears smear my vision, or is it the cloudy breath that rolls up her face? She wears the thick black coat, the one that walked me to school yesterday. A few gray hairs dance above her eyes, freed from her black kerchief, its small knot under her chin choking her.

My body aches to get off the train, to clutch the scratchy wool coat, to hear the singsong of her chatter. I want to break the glass. I want to sit in the kitchen. I want her to wipe my runny nose. I don't want the ten years of my Annus left on the platform.

I cringe against my mother's grip on my shoulder, her words a slap in my ears. I don't know where the train is taking us. I don't want to know.

AUSTRIA

1957–1969

New Foods *1957*
Lainzerstrasse 60 *March 1957*
Israel *1958*
Milk Jug *1960*
Music *1962*
My Secret *1966*

New Foods

Ten years old

In Vienna the streetcars are red.
Why not yellow like at home?
Too many questions squeeze my chest.

Cold sneaks in through the window.
The three of us huddle in a hotel room.
Gloves, socks and underwear dry on the radiator,
Where occasional hisses disrupt the quiet.
Outside, the February snow
Swept off the sidewalk, shimmers with wetness.

A hear a knock on the door.
I remember that man.
A large brown paper bag in one hand,
The other hugs my parents.
He makes room on the table, calls me to look.

Oranges, bananas, chocolates.
He names each one as he empties the bag.
I hold the round, bumpy orange and shrug.
"We have to peel it."
He peels it with his bare hands,
Unfolds a ball that's lost its cover
And breaks it into segments.
"Taste it." He puts one in my mouth.
Is this sweet or sour?
Can I swallow the whole thing?

My mother grabs a banana.
I recognize it from pictures.
"We have to peel it."
She pulls the yellow outside halfway down,
Tells me to take a bite of the white stuff.
Sticky and dry,
It turns into mushy paste in my mouth.

Too embarrassed to spit it out,
I turn back to the window.
I long for the apple my Annus used to
Cut into small slices.
A red streetcar rumbles past.

Lainzerstrasse 60

Vienna, March 1957
Ten years old

I

Street noises rattle the quiet,
My only companion in the room.
The dirty lace curtain
Cannot hide the outside.
Women, bundled up in long black coats,
Hair hidden under kerchiefs and scarves,
Their gloved fingers clutch handles of shopping nets.
Shapeless items, covered in newspaper
Lie atop each other like sardines in a can.
Their weight pulls the women forward.
Heads bent, eyes search the icy sidewalk.

A red streetcar screeches to its stop,
Black metal tracks lonely next to the curb.
A shiver turns me around.

I walk to the warmth of the *Kachelofen*,
Sit down on the carpet.
The stove's tall columns of square green tiles
March from floor to ceiling,
My hand sweeps along their surface.
Inside each tile lies a hollowed circle,
Like an empty eye socket.
My fingers bump from tile to tile,
Along the shiny smoothness.

I try to count them — there are too many.
I stay on the carpet, comforted by mute heat.

My mother's whisper plays in my head. The landlady said,
"I have more of these carpets in the attic,
They belonged to some Jews."
Jews, Juden, zsidok — words new to me,
They float around, playing catch with the dust motes.
A secret I can't decode.

II

A cold March wind squeezes between my parents and me,
Helps push open the heavy door.
Nothing here looks like my old school.
My old school was in that other place.
Will anyone speak Hungarian in this 4th grade?

We walk up a long staircase.
Questions and fears swarm,
New and strange
Like the language that awaits me.
My heart pounds through our footsteps,
Disturbs the echo of the stillness,
Until our silent ascent ends.

"Here in Vienna all children must attend religion classes.
You will be enrolled as Protestant.
You must keep it a secret."
And on we walk — up the steps.

Israel

Eleven years old

I

EL AL airlines carries me to a new country,
Streetcars and trains left in Vienna.

In a few hours we land in Israel.
Israel — a word I only heard at home,
Seen on postage stamps and envelopes
Quickly discarded.
Israel, where I'll meet relatives
Whose names swirl in my mind
Like the scribble on the papers
That traveled in the envelopes.

For years relatives were faceless story-people
On a spot I can barely find on the map.
A secret place,
Known only to the three of us.

II

My cousin Mira teaches me to count in Hebrew.
Echad, shtein, shalosh . . .

In a dark room, too hot, musty,
I look at an old man,
My grandfather Saba,
They tell me.

Wrapped in an eiderdown,
I swing in a hammock.
Unfamiliar aromas dance
From my aunt Ella's kitchen,
And spread their sweet warmth.

Her daughter Hannah grabs my hand.
We run down the street,
She sings a Hebrew song,
Urges me on
With the few Hungarian words she knows.

With my parents
I go from home to home.
I count the people.
Echad, shtein, shalosh.
Every day there are more.
Voices, languages seduce, implore,
Vie to be first.

Hands embrace me,
A comfort so new,
Strangers only days ago,
Now so familiar.

Among them I run faster,
Talk louder – grow taller.

The shushing and hush of Budapest,
The secrets and curtsies of Vienna
Now abhorred.
I plead, I cry, I beg to stay.

The chorus of my relatives
Echoes my hope.

My parents' verdict, "No."

III

The airplane seat sticks to me,
My legs dangle leaden.
They ripped me away from my Annus,
They ripped me away from my new family.

I swallow screams that crawl through my chest.
The sky dissolves in the belly of a cloud.
My father murmurs,
His cigarette breath sweeps my face.
My mother's Lake Balaton eyes silent,
Her lips lock up all sound.

Milk Jug

Thirteen years old

The cold metal container sways in my hand. Hitting my knee, its hollowness startles me. After a few more bangings we move to a rhythm, the milk jug and my knee. The steep dirt road is empty. The meadow absorbs the gravel rolling around. The deer I see on my morning walks must be grazing behind the trees.

My little duet stops as I get to the main road. The farmhouse is on the other side. The cars let me cross.

How did Mary know I am at her door? She greets me curtly, her thin voice drones in my ear, her calloused hand unclenches my fist. I wait for her to bring the jug back. It's heavy now. I can't resume our little duet.

I walk back up the dirt road carefully, so the milk doesn't spill. It's just the three of us — the jug, the milk and me. Quiet accompanies us home. The door is ajar, my mother calls from the kitchen. She hugs me. I still hold the jug. She slowly takes it from me.

"Was Mary happy to see you?"

I shrug and sit down, my little duet still playing in my head. I watch my mother's quick dance with the milk jug — on the counter, lid off, skimming the top of the milk into a big bowl. The metal whisk clanks against the ceramic, her hand draws small circles in the air and a dense white cloud appears.

The aroma of hot cocoa on the stove warms me. She fills my cup with the chocolaty liquid, sweetened with four sugar cubes and spoons the whipped cream over it. My mother sits down next to me, watches me lick off the sweet, brown remnants all around my lips.

Her eyes hold many questions. I don't know which one to answer.

Music

Fifteen years old

My parents quietly look up as I walk into the living room. As usual, classical music plays on the radio. Rock 'n Roll lurks at the Austrian border, impatient for an entry visa. Not content with only Mozart, Haydn and Schubert, the Viennese stubbornly claim Beethoven as their own.

New Year's Eve is Strauss's night. The waltz rules over the twist.

"Do you know what this is?" My father's chestnut eyes kind, expectant. A derisive smile fleetingly crosses his soft cheeks.
"It's Bach," I say, bravura hiding the hesitancy in my voice.
"No, Bach is never this playful. It's Vivaldi."

My father turns his head. I watch the cigarette smoke swirl up from lips now hidden from me. Indignation belies my humiliation. Anger swallows my sadness.

Decades later, continents away, I sit in a concert hall in Los Angeles. The program's Baroque chamber music includes Vivaldi and Bach. Yes, Vivaldi is playful but only Bach quivers my soul.

As the music recedes, I flip through my mind's Rolodex searching for the one who should sit next to me. That page is blank. Years have passed, languages accumulated, landscapes changed.

Bach and Vivaldi are mine alone.

My Secret

Nineteen years old

My acquired language sounds like them.
And yet, they detect
My otherness so easily.

What they don't see (but seem to sense)
Is tucked away – my secret.
An unutterable truth, all mine.
I am its loyal guardian.

At times the secret tries to
Drip out of my mouth.
I push it away – continue to
Traverse the hazy make-believe.

Finally, of legal age,
I crave to flee to freedom.
My armor, the secret keeper,
Is ready to burst.

I spit it out to Eva, my friend of many years.
"I am Jewish."
My sweaty fingers stir the spoon in the espresso,
Long after the sugar has dissolved.

Offering up my true identity,
Eva's smile caresses my face,
Her voice gentle,
"I always knew."

PHOBOS

Phobos

Birds *1969*

Phobos

My uninvited companion
Spreads its claws, grips all thought.
The steady stream may leak some chunks
Lost in unknown territory.

Thick black blood slogs,
Its invisible master relentless.
Loud, determined to spill over
Or just to push the walls
Beyond their tracks.

I beg to grasp this sudden invasion,
Its secret plan a dark cloud.
My chest heaves to a foreign rhythm
Pounding through gasping breaths,
My brain a panicked fog.

Fear unleashed –
Squeezes, thrashes, strangles.
Phobos rules.

Birds

The sand warm against my back,
My bare heels dig into its softness.
Bathing in the warmth of the sun,
I hear the waves' secret melody,
Too far to intrude on my solitude.

A flock of black geese assaults
The sharp blue of the immense sky.
Their flapping and shrill honking
An excruciating noise.
Panic slithers through my body.
A family trait ingrained in me,
This fear of flying creatures,
Claws at me — leaves my body rigid.

The whoosh of wings and screeches fades.
I watch the birds follow an invisible path,
Their shapes morph into black boots, shiny, loud.
Heels first, in perfect unison.
I see the horde of polished leather,
Synchronized with ghastly sound.
The roar and rhythm of heel to heel
Cannot obscure the whip rising from the boot.
Its thong twists in the air,
Its howl keeps tempo with the stomping men,
The cement cracks, pebbles fly,
Crushed by its lash.

An endless march, a steady flow of blackness.
It leaves a quiet in a foreign language,
A language only the cement answers to.
They pass, but already I hear
The rumblings of another group,
The drone of goose steps, the falsetto of the whip,
A hypnotic throb of terror.

The birds continue on their flight
Keeping track, not looking back.
Slowly they disappear, the sky remains.
I feel the wetness of the sand stick to my legs,
It rains out of my hair.
I start walking away from the birds.
I carry the fear with me,
Hopes left in my footprints.

AMERICA

1969 – present

Love — Mistaken
Twenty-two years old

I feel him — who is that? I get on the streetcar, can't find a seat. Now I see him, he comes close. "You are in my psych class." I don't remember him. He looks so nondescript. I hear his words, some stick, some I lose.

We sip espresso, smoke L&Ms, blend with students escaping the cold autumn afternoon. He tells me his name — Horst, from the South. We drink more coffee, feast on Sartre, Nietzsche and Freud. We see French movies, listen to Mozart, Bach and the Beatles.

We march in protest of the Viet Nam War. Make love, have sex, fight.

With each month, season, our bubble thickens. He adores me, I love to be adored.

I meet his parents, the father who was a Nazi — because it was the war. He meets my parents. My mother shudders thinking of her family in Israel. His mother says nothing, all questions tied up in her apron.

He spoils me, he worships me. I feed on his love, bathe in his adoration. I wear the ring he gives me when we are together. I am his queen like my mother is to my father, my idol. I let him atone for his father's sins. We both silently accept our roles.

Two years later I leave Vienna, promise my parents to join them, promise Horst to be back. Letters cross the Atlantic filled with tales of love and longing. He keeps his pledge and comes to America. We meet in secret. I see him, this nondescript, small-town figure. I don't need him anymore.

I slip the silver band off my finger and toss it in the heap of mistakes.

I break his heart — I shatter his dream. I am cruel, I am me. I am free.

Love

Twenty-five years old

I've known him only a few weeks,
His body so familiar,
His thoughts a boundless surprise.
He pulls the covers over our heads,
Our bodies' heat dries the sex-wet skin.

My face melts into his voice.
He tells me of his grandfather
Sitting in *shul*,
The *tallit* enfolding them both.
The aged calloused hand
Ready with candy,
His Russian English
Sweetened by silent caress.

This memory that isn't mine
Floods through me like warm lava,
And I behold my grandfather
I saw only once.
He too prayed in *shul.*
His voice tender yet remote,
The numbers etched on his forearm
Recount a secret past.

Under the covers
My lover offers his deepest self,
Filled with trust and truth.
I decode it, I clench it.
He reads my wordless heart.

Reunion

Twenty-six years old

I stumble on the cobblestones,
I hear my footsteps, see the little girl
Hold her nanny's hand walking to her home.
The streets, the houses, the trees,
The passersby, the other language,
Now shadows from the past.
"Are you nervous?" my husband asks.
"Are you worried?"

Words float up I don't connect,
Shapeless thoughts I can't decipher.
I don't feel anxious, I don't feel excited,
I am astonished I don't feel anything.
"Here is where I walked with Annus,
This is where she scolded me to look both ways
Before crossing the street."
I keep looking. I keep talking.

We open the creaky wooden gate,
Traipse through the front yard.
How long ago did they plant this?
Yes, it's the same heavy brown door.
There she is my Annus –
My nanny, my mother, my love, my happy memory.
She is tiny and chubby, sparse gray hair
Surrounds her round face.
A big smile unveils missing teeth.

Her strong arms enfold me,
Her kisses swallow my tears.
Hungarian pours over my husband,
Who doesn't understand her words
But later plays them all back to me.

I bring my present and future into the room
Where the walls still whisper a child's secrets.
I zigzag through time zones,
I translate, choke on my words.
I hold Annus's hand, the hand now smaller than mine,
That held the handkerchief so I could blow my nose,
That cooked endless meals and laced up my shoes.
The hand I couldn't reach sixteen years ago,
As I leaned out the train window,
Uncomprehending that she would not come with me.

And now I am back.
I try to sit in the chair not like a visitor,
Not like the little girl from long ago.
Questions mingle with stories,
Oceans dry up between continents.
We toss memory pieces like ping pong balls,
Their echo will soften the distance.

First Birth

Twenty-eight years old

My sweat and smile
Still her cry,
I kiss her almost-hair.
My fingers tremble above her cheek,
Her heartbeat a steady gallop
Against my swollen breast.
My eyes feast on the warm softness
I nurtured for so long.

I imagine the umbilical cord roaming
In my now empty womb –
A pendulum set loose.

Scenes of her future
Assault my mind,
The will to protect her
Claws at me,
Possessiveness – a surprise.

Her eyes still blind,
Her smile a reflex,
My arms a soft cushion.
Our competing breaths
Seep through a fragile cocoon.

Bedtime

Thirty-eight years old

She waits for me.
Her favorite pink nightgown
Peeks out from the puffy eiderdown.
Lumpy hills in a white meadow
Hint at a small child's body.
"Mommy, sit down,"
The dim glow from the Minnie Mouse nightlight
Guides me to her bed.
The noises from behind the closed door a faraway murmur.
We both relish our bedtime togetherness.
She lies on her side, chin cradled in her palm.
Velvet blue eyes wide open,
Her long chestnut hair spread like branches of willow
Across the pillow.
She pulls her arm from under the cover,
Taps the empty space next to her.
I sit down – hold her outstretched hand.
She asks questions, tells tidbits from her day.
She scatters memory morsels, squeezes my fingers greedily.
"Time to go to sleep, my munchkin."
"No, not yet, Mommy."
She holds tight, eyes wide open begging.
I bathe in her love, in her neediness.
I stay. I pull my hand out of her grip.
"It's really time to go to sleep."
"Can't you just cut your hand off?"
Her innocence fills the silence.

She is so seductive in her desire to hold onto me.
I fall for her sweet voice, pleading eyes,
Her soft fingers caressing my knuckles.
I hear her playfulness, feel her fear.
I see the ghosts dancing in the room,
Waiting for her to fly with them.
She is enchanting and tender. I swallow my sadness.
My hand freed — I stroke her head, kiss her silky cheek.

PARENTS

Mother

Eyes battle for amber or emerald,
Chiseled nose enveloped by Slavic cheekbones.

Lips still when *numerus clausus*
Forces her to clean others' homes.
With quiet rage
She nurses her mother to her death.
She survives Bergen-Belsen.
Faith in peace emboldens her
To follow her man,
To leave her family behind.

She bears a child,
Witnesses her husband's disappearance.
She waits years to flee again,
Tanks trample a promising future.

She yields to new countries,
New languages.
Her lips guard fury and fear.
To object, resist, demand
Is *verboten.*

Hitler and Stalin remembered,
Religion abandoned,
Curiosity lost.
She obeys the puppeteer's strings.

Yitgadal v'yitkadash sh'mey raba
B'alma di v'ra khirutey,
She doesn't mourn,
She doesn't pray,
No hope, no tears,
She dies bereft of speech.

Farewell

He is gone.
Cigarette's pungent smell fleeing,
Its smoke triumphs over Hitler's chimney's stacks.
The Magic Mountain unclimbed,
Marx and the new world unfinished.
Espressos downed,
Oceans crossed,
Ideas debated.
Connective tissue torn,
Shadows claw at my soul.
Random images invade my reality.
I cling to the void.
I cry for him.

The Last Goodbye

I am going back. Back to a place that is home only as a memory, a language stunted decades ago. I had anticipated my father's death for years. The expectation now a fact – the imagined loss a deep pain.

The last one who knew the child and the adult, gone. The last one to share my mother tongue will not talk again.

I am going back to feel his thoughts, breathe his words stacked on bookshelves, smell his cigarettes in the yellowed curtains.

Will I now put the idealized image next to the dead body? How can I safeguard my core with its mirror image buried? I know the backside of the mirror, the dark silver reflecting that which is hidden. The disdain, narcissism, stubbornness, all real. And yet I understood. And forgave. And loved.

The orphaned room will receive me. I will touch the air, breathe the smell, listen in the quiet – call him.

MOTHER'S & FATHER'S FAMILY

Tuli and Zsuzsa

Winter 1943
Streets yearn for their citizens.
Bombs and sirens hunt soldiers.
The wounded, the bodies wait
To heal or to die.

Zsuzsa wears a nurse's coat,
Its buttons pop off like faraway bullets,
Leaving her cleavage to soothe hungry eyes.
The hospital safer than the safe house
Where she and her mother hide.

Her young poet husband,
Gunned down, thrown into the Danube.
For two years, the young lovers survived,
Read poetry and illegal fliers,
Listened to Bach and Janáček.

Her father, whose favorite child she was,
Picked up on the streets of Budapest – disappeared,
Joined her husband in the purple waters of the river?
Two men vanished,
Pebbles among the 200,000 Jews of Budapest,
Sand kernels of the 500,000 of Hungary.

Spring 1944
She saves her mother from the Romanian soldier
Who walks into her apartment.
"Leave her alone, I am better, I promise."

He is young, eager. He likes what he is offered.
He retreats with a smile, never returns.

Summer 1944
"Hey, pretty one."
She lifts the blanket.
There lies a skinny, healthy, uninjured body.
His deep baritone a stark contrast to thin voices of the sick.
Under the soiled frayed blanket
She nods to a square chin and wide cheekbones.
She quickly gauges he is not Hungarian.
Eyes like polished black shoe leather hold her tight.
She knows, just knows, here is a Jew, hiding.
He plays another round of roulette — he trusts her.
Weary of his brazen flirting,
She is awed by his bold maneuver into a hospital bed.

A few days later he is gone.
He finds her.
He brings her food, chocolates, and his body.
Their hungers sated, her mind aches for her poet husband.
She no longer discusses art, music, literature.
Her bourgeois undone.

She welcomes the stranger.
Tuli, a *yeshiva bocher*,
Fled from a *shtetl* in Transylvania,
Left his father in the butcher shop.
He yearned to get away from the smell of animal blood
And meat hanging from hooks.
He moves West, joins the resistance in Budapest.

Fall 1944
The earth is still soft enough,
The freedom fighters dig a hole in an empty field.
They scheme, steal, feed on luck.
Soon they disperse.
He knows about the murders, the deportations.
A contact tells him his brother is at the train station.
He puts on the German uniform he wore
When he scoured for food and water.
He dirties the black boots and his clothes,
Confident that it hides the Jew.
He searches for hours. He goes back alone.

Spring 1945
Russians free the country.
His anti-fascist belief does not extend
To the socialist communist promise.
Homes and families a memory,
With Zsuzsa he follows the refugee trek.

Fall 1945
In Paris they unite with his siblings.
The *yeshiva* boy struggles to survive.
He smuggles watches inside hollowed out salami.
He trades, he hustles.

Spring 1946
They marry.
He for love,
She for the silent call in her womb.

Fall 1954

They leave, in search for new hope,
Cross the ocean to join family in Los Angeles.
He builds her a life of luxury.
She teaches him about art and music and literature.

Wealth shrouds their scars.
Forever he asks questions and grieves for an answer.
Forever she misses the two men she once loved.

She and I

Her namesake, her mirror,
She anoints me her successor.
Her daughter and other nieces cast aside.

Genes migrate,
Our similarities abound.

Proudly, the gypsy aristocrat
Flaunts the old world.
Zest for the now propels her,
Closes the door to coffins.

Her father lost to Hitler's henchmen,
My father vanished to Stalin's deputies.
Quest for brutal disappearances
Traverses generations.
Images disrupt sleep,
Unanswered questions hover.

Our willful disregard to conform
Induces envy and contempt.
The shrug of a shoulder silences words.
Unrestrained love for the elected few
Softens haughtiness and narcissism.

Money welcome but not esteemed.
Culture, our crown.
Confidence and arrogance
Elevate art and beauty to a deity.
With *noblesse oblige* we envelop our world.

I abandon fear of freedom,
I surrender to life.
Our footsteps embrace
In the echo from afar.

Waiting Room

I am a visitor, an outsider
In a room filled with people waiting,
Pacing, sleeping, whispering,
Righting a wig,
A kerchief, a knitted cap, a brimmed hat.

I am an intruder, an onlooker
In a room filled with hungry cells,
Dead cells, cells asleep, cells fighting.
Eyes stare begging to know,
Lips shut to swallow the fear.
Worn out bodies silent, starved for hope,
Filled with fortitude.

A voice calls out names, room numbers.
A jumble of dreams and despair
Vanishes inside the white walled cubicles.
Hours crawl with a hush,
Empty chairs quickly fill again.
The room echoes with mute terror,
Swaddled in faith for tomorrow.

Orit, My Cousin

I came to see you,
I came to see you one more time,
The last time.

Sunset reflects in windows far off,
Windows glisten like golden eyes.
Evergreens stand tall,
Indifferent to seasons.
The steady highway rumble,
An ignorant noise,
Cannot veil the rasp of your breath.

Your bloated body, a stranger to this bed.
Your voice shriveled to a faint whisper.
Gobs of bloodstained mucous
Spew through your wounded throat
Until it flows easily,
A bright red liquid,
An unstoppable river
Where your breath drowns.

You were my sister,
The one I yearned for,
And I will not have another sister again.

CELLO

1943 – present

Cello

First Movement
1943

Pál's arm hangs loosely over the top of his cello. The familiar dissonance of German, French and Hungarian fill the room. Friends and strangers toast with wine and vodka for France to defeat Hitler. The room brims with youthful illusion and confidence. Cheers, dancing and laughter mask their worry.

The cello rests against Pál's leg. Together they traveled from Budapest to Berlin, on to Brussels and Paris. Now in Toulouse, they exalt in a celebration of freedom and hope.

Liszt's "Csárdás" resounds from the piano. The *allegro vivace* spurs the dancers on. Pál grabs the cello by its neck, holds it up high and joins in. He swirls and turns, faster and faster. The bow in his hand swings wildly, the strings immobile. The music races to rhythmic clapping and shouts of *liberté, égalité, frat...*

The cello slips, tumbles, splinters. Strings like pickup sticks spread in all directions. Pál falls. His long fingers trace the scattered pieces of wood.

The pianist begins to play Liszt's "Totentanz". Its slow, mournful *andante* echoes the stalled gaiety in the room. Pál strokes the hairs on the bow, its smoothness a mute solace. He lifts it like a magic wand, places it in the empty case.

As weeks pass, Pál spends endless hours in his small rented room. Music only he can hear bounces off the peeling paint. The empty cello case yearns to be filled.

A loud knock on the door disrupts the quiet. Pál strains to listen for boot steps but hears only the pounding of his heart. Fear glues him to the chair.

"It's me, Jan," a voice repeats.

Pál's sweaty palm slips off the door handle. He tries again. The door opens. His brother-in-law, Jan, a patron of the arts, passes a new cello case to him. It weighs heavily in Pál's trembling hand. He looks around, lays it gently on the bed.

Pál stares at Jan, obeys his nod, opens it. An unuttered question burns in Pál's eyes. He shudders at Jan's hushed words.

"It's a Gagliano. For you."

Cello

Second Movement
1944

A different music is heard in Toulouse – the guttural "France" now only whispered. Strident Deutsch sweeps the empty streets.

Hunched on the bicycle, Jan zigzags through deserted alleys. Pál's lamenting melody hushes his fears. Pál, his brother-in-law, is now one of the disappeared.

Jan pedals, the cello sings. Darkness warns as the sky sheds its orange. At the gate, the concierge blinks and wordlessly hands him Pál's key.

Jan's farm boots obey the tiptoe command. He heaves at the sight of the sealed door. His heart hammers staring at the swastika stamps. The knife used to cut bread and cheese, now labors quickly to free the entrance.

Jan tightens his lips, swallows a shout. Only the cello, leaning against the wall, witnesses the laughter in his eyes. He grabs the instrument, carefully closes the door. He counts the steps to quiet his mind, slides past the concierge and mounts his bike. The almost dark carries him back to the farm.

Cello
Third Movement
1944 – present

The orphaned cello waits, silent in the darkness. No light sneaks into its coffin case. Strangers' voices raise hope to hear its sound.

The SNCF rumbles, jerks at each stop. Vilmos who filled Pál's empty chair in the "Hungarian Quartet" hears the train's whistle and steadies the cello between his legs.

Trees, towns and meadows speed by, bleed into Vilmos's vision of Convoy # 73 of the Deutsche Bundesbahn that carried Pál to his unmarked grave.

Did Pál tell of his love for Ada Weever, the young Dutch *beauté*? Did he tell of how she drowned? Did he tell how his little daughter is now safe in Holland?

Vilmos tosses memories out the train window. France slides past. Land flattens as Holland nears.

"*Welcom in onze familie.*" Voices, faces cling to Vilmos, the forlorn understudy. He searches for Pál in the girl, her upturned palm the only question. He unites the orphaned cello with the fifteen-year-old orphan Corrie.

Her fingers walk across the black case probing for a smell, a sound – the drowned, a storybook mother, the disappeared father, blurry sepia pictures. Their absence a silent cry in her ear to greet the ones to whom she couldn't say good-bye. Losses, wounds in Corrie's young heart, will swim in her veins in search for answers.

Corrie finds a new guardian for the cello, makes room for her family. Her first child, Ada, a legacy to the one the North Sea swallowed.

Pali, her youngest, is heir to the name and the musical gift. His honeyed baritone saturates concert halls that once belonged to the other Pál.

The composer's ghost whispers to young Pali who restlessly traverses his grandfather's footsteps gathering bits of scores ignored by Hitler's henchmen.

The music sheets flutter as he hums notes that dance up and down the staff lines. His voice soars, he roams and collects, assembles the broken pieces.

Pál's body vanished, its unseen blood a river of rebirth, in which music once bemoaned for lost, floats into a new century, travels across continents, tells stories unfettered, never to be silenced again.

Cello

Fourth Movement
A New Century

Following the death of my father and his sister (the nephew and niece of Pál the composer) a void haunted me. In 2017, to keep the Hermann family name alive, we created the Susan and Murray Brown Endowment Fund in Honor and Memory of Cellist Pál Hermann at the Colburn School in Los Angeles.

The almost lost notes float from Italy to America, where Pali (Pál's grandson) joins the cachet of "Recovered Voices". A first performance in 2018 enchants the Colburn Academy of Music. More and more scores grow into a complete cello concerto, delight performers and audiences from Lvov to Seattle, from concert halls to CDs, from program notes to the web.

A voice, once forbidden and extinguished, is reborn and enriches the musical world.

Pál's legacy lives on assured by his heirs.

CIRCLES

I wander — seek to fill a nameless void,
Soothe a faceless ache.
For years I nurture,
I give, I hope, I lie.
But the absence finds me,
Pushes and persists.

I surrender — crush my wall,
Exclaim shalom,
Free the shadows.
And travel to my remembered home.

Cigarette smell squeezed between stacks of books,
Some penned by authors known,
Some by one known only to a few.

I take my father's tattered dictionary
That helped tell his stories in many lands.
I take it,
Give it a new life.

Longing and searches becalmed,
I write stories.
The dictionary and I
Tell tales that others lived.
Someone will find them,
And add them to their own.

APPENDIX

History of Name Changes

Frigyes (my grandfather) and Pál Hermann (his brother) were born at the turn of the 19th century in Budapest, Hungary.

In 1945, Frigyes's son (my father) György (Gyuri) assimilated back to Hungary and changed his name to Hódos. In Austria, he changed it Georg Hodos, in the US to George Hodos.

Márta Friedländer (my mother) hid under the alias Forgács until deported. She married my father George and took his name.

In 1939, Pál moved his Dutch wife Ada and their daughter Corrie to safety in Holland. Corrie's youngest son Pali carried on the musical talent of his grandfather. His Italian wife adopted his name, Van Gastel.

Wars, expulsions, escapes.
Borders and politics like porous banners,
Names, countries, identities
In constant change.

. . .

Pál Hermann — b. 1902 Budapest, Hungary, d. 1944 Kaunas, Lithuania

Frigyes Hermann — b. 1891 Budapest, Hungary, d. 1944 Dachau, Germany

György Hermann — b. 1921 Budapest, Hungary > György Hódos (1946) > Georg Hodos (1957 Austria) > George Hodos (1969 US), d. 2015

Márta Friedländer — b. 1917 Nagybakta, Hungary > Márta Forgács (1944) > Márta Hódos (1946) > Martha Hodos (1957, Austria) > Martha Hodos (1969 US), d. 1994

Zsuzsi Hódos — b. 1947 Budapest, Hungary > Susi Hodos (1957, Austria) > Susan Hodos (1969 US) > Susan Brown (1973)

Zsuzsa Hermann — b. 1922 Budapest, Hungary > Zsuzsa Rosenberg (1946) > Susan Roland (1955 US), d. 2014

ACKNOWLEDGEMENTS

In memory of my mother — for teaching me the value of loyalty, self-reliance and a healthy skepticism.

In memory of my father — for showing me the beauty in music and the written word, and the importance of idealism, persistence and the hope for a better world.

Thank you to Deborah Edler Brown, the first to encourage my foray into writing.

With deep gratitude to Martha Fuller, whose skill and patience guided me through the process of creating this legacy.

A special recognition for two books that accompanied me on this journey.

Hodos, George H. *Show Trials: Stalinist Purges in Eastern Europe, 1948-1954.* Praeger Publishers, A Division of Greenwood Press, Inc., 1987

Lendvai, Paul. *The Hungarians: A Thousand Years of Victory in Defeat.* Princeton University Press, 2003

SUSAN H. BROWN

Born in Budapest, Hungary in 1947, Susan H. Brown moved to Vienna, Austria in 1957 and emigrated to the US in 1969. In 1973 she received an MA from Boston University, (German Languages and Literature) and in 1987 she received an MA from California State University, Northridge (Communication Disorders). She lives in Los Angeles, California where she works as a speech/language therapist.

This book is typeset in Bembo, an old-style humanist serif typeface originally cut by Francesco Griffo in 1495 and revived by Stanley Morison in 1929. Display type is Futura.

CPSIA information can be obtained
at www.ICGtesting.com
Printed in the USA
JSHW011933100223
37567JS00007B/121